Living in Freedom

Living in Freedom

The Abundant Life

Stan DeKoven, Ph.D.

Copyright ©2012 Stan E. DeKoven

ISBN 978-1-61529-031-4

Vision Publishing

1672 Main Street, E109

Ramona, CA 92065

1 800-9-VISION

www.booksbyvision.com

All rights are reserved internationally except for brief comments in articles, etc. and only by permission of the author.

Contents

Introduction   **1**
     Context, Context, Context   3

1   Freedom from What and for What?   **7**
     Freedom Defined   7
     Start With Where You Look and Where You Sit   8
     Fully Alive   11

2   Freedom is Being Who You Are   **15**
     Consider it   21
     I AM   22
     Paul's Echo   23

3   Keep Looking Up!   **27**
     Man in the Mirror   30
     A Tough Place   30

4   Freedom through the Anointing   **35**
     We Got It   37

5   Conclusion   **39**
     A Final Thought for Leaders Present and Future   40

About the Author   **43**

Some Other Books by Dr. Stan DeKoven   **45**

"In almost everything that touches our everyday life on earth, God is pleased when we're pleased. He wills that we be as free as birds to soar and sing our maker's praise without anxiety." —A.W. Tozer

"Remember, you may choose your sin, but you cannot choose the consequences."
—Jenny Sanford

Introduction

In the year 2011, it was my privilege to present a series of messages to a dynamic church in Fontana California; Fontana Christian Fellowship International, pastored by Gary and Gina Holly. This year's sermon series was titled Freedom in Christ: Living the Abundant Life. Living a Christian life is not always easy. In fact, some say it's impossible for us to live the Christian life. All we can do is allow the life of Christ, which is essentially Jesus himself, to become fully expressed through us. In many ways, that is the theme of this booklet.

Finding true freedom in Christ does not come by our self-effort or by great striving. It does not come by our first class prayer or by our intense study in the word of God, although all of these things are good. In fact, we live the life of Christ by allowing Christ to live his life through us, where he fully expresses the heart of a loving Father to the world. Thus, it is my hope that as God gives grace, this small book will be a blessing to many in the body of Christ who struggle with the concept of freedom.

What is freedom and how do we fully gain the inheritance of the abundant life Christ has obtained for us, by his death, burial, resurrection and ascension? We know that Christ is seated at the right hand of the Father in glory, and that we are seated with him in the spirit. We

Introduction

are far above principalities and powers, living in righteousness, peace and joy in the Holy Spirit... now.

It is inherent for every believer to find their role in the life of the church, and to find out what the word of God says about this important concept. It is fully discussed by Paul in Second Corinthians...

> "For the Lord is the spirit and where the Spirit of the Lord is there is liberty. But we all with unveiled face beholding as in a mirror the glory of the Lord are being transformed into the same image from glory to glory just as from the Lord; the Spirit"
> —2 Corinthians 3:17-18

In the context of Paul's writing in First Corinthians, he teaches specifically on the greater glory found in Christ, rather than the glory found in Moses and the Ten Commandments. He provides a contrast to the glory of the Old Covenant depicted here as seen in the face of Moses. Moses covered his face when coming down the mountain from his encounter with God. It was not because God's glory was too magnificent, but rather because the glory (that is the light reflected from the face of Moses) had faded after he left the Lord's presence. There was glory in the Old Covenant, but not the same level of glory we find in the New Covenant in Christ through the shedding of his blood.

You could say what is contrasted here is the difference between the outer presence of God; or his glory, goodness and grace with the inner presence of God. (This is a concept that will be defined more clearly later in this text.) It is the awareness and the reality that by the Holy Spirit, Christ lives in us. He is expressing who he is through us, both as individuals and within the body of Christ.

Context, Context, Context

Paul's teaching on the greater glory in Christ is the context, and the problematic but powerful church in Corinth was his audience. Through Christ and by Holy Spirit, Paul presents the potent benefits of life in the Spirit (Pneuma, breath, presence) which includes;

- Life Without Barriers. This does not mean I can do my own thing, living only for the moment; but it does mean a life that is open and without guilt, and especially without shame.

For in fact, as we look into the face of Christ, which we do through the disciplines of the study of the word, worship, service and prayer, our face is lifted. It is a true face-lift, not the Hollywood version. It not only provides an outward freedom, but is also a true lifting of our perspective from self and the world, to Christ and his divine purposes. As we look unto Jesus, who is the author and the completer of our faith, the one who for our own benefit transforms us from the inside out, we are truly changed. (Hebrews 12:1-2) Further...

- His freedom allows us to be filled with all the fullness of God. This includes his life, light, love, and our praise or our Doxa, for his honor or glory.

In light of this, we can and should expect that as we live in relationship with the Lord, we will see complete liberation from the past, our sin, sickness, fear, etc., as this is the plan of God for us, as described in Isaiah 61 and Luke 4.

"The Spirit of the Lord GOD is upon me; because the LORD has anointed me to bring

Introduction

> good news to the afflicted, He has sent me to bind up the brokenhearted, to proclaim liberty to the captives, and freedom to prisoners; to proclaim the favorable[1] year of the Lord."
>
> —Luke 4:18-19

This liberty or freedom refers to the great Jubilee God provided for the children of Israel although they rarely if ever practiced it. It included the cancelling of all debts, allowing families to start over once again. What a joy this would be, a divinely planned bankruptcy and an opportunity to start over! In practical terms, this was good news indeed! The law of Jubilee is found in Leviticus...

> "You shall thus consecrate the fiftieth year and proclaim a release through the land to all its inhabitants. I shall be a jubilee for you, and each of you shall return to his own property and each of you will return to his family." —Leviticus 25:10

The Jubilee discussed in the Old Testament, with all of its glory, was just a foreshadowing of the glory God has provided for us in Christ, under the New Covenant. God's plan was activated in the death, burial, resurrection and ascension of Christ. He did this for his children, so they may live in true freedom. The purpose is to transform us into the very image of Christ, so that we can be and do all for God, our families, and for our society; as God ordained us to be and do from the beginning (see Genesis 1:26). The question is this, what is freedom? How can we experience the abundant life promised by Jesus in John 10:10? That is the subject of this booklet.

---

[1] And, in Isaiah, the day of vengeance; but this is left out of Jesus' reading as recorded in Luke 4.

"Either sin is with you, lying on your shoulders, or it is lying on Christ, the Lamb of God. Now if it is lying on your back, you are lost; but if it is resting on Christ, you are free, and you will be saved.
Now choose what you want."
—Martin Luther

"God's terrible insistence on human freedom is so absolute that he granted us the power to live as though He did not exist, to spit in His face, to crucify Him."
—Philip Yancey[2]

---

[2] *The Jesus I Never Knew*, Zondervan, 1995

Chapter 1

Freedom from What and for What?

Freedom Defined

This brief definition is taken from Dictionary.com
   Lib·er·ty is defined as 1. Freedom from arbitrary or despotic government or control. 2. Freedom from external or foreign rule; independence. 3. Freedom from control, interference, obligation, restriction, hampering conditions, etc.; power or right of doing, thinking, speaking, etc., according to choice. 4. Freedom from captivity, confinement, or physical restraint: The prisoner soon regained his liberty.
   Freedom, also taken from Dictionary.com is 1. The state of being free or at liberty rather than in confinement or under physical restraint: He won his freedom after a retrial. 2. Exemption from external control, interference, regulation, etc. 3. The power to determine action without restraint. 4. Political or national independence. 5. Personal liberty, as opposed to bondage or slavery: a slave who bought his freedom.

Freedom from What and for What?

As one can easily see, the definitions are strikingly similar, almost word for word with rare exception. The concept of freedom seems to encompass the ability to make one's own choices within the general societal rules or propriety, and without external constraints, whether political or otherwise. I would add to this that freedom or liberty is defined within the confines of moral freedom, or freedom to be who we were intended to be, as defined by God and his word, properly understood. Freedom to do whatever one wants, without the necessary restraints of natural or judicial law, which is anarchy, would not be a part of my definition.

This type of "freedom" leads to chaos, which is not the will of God, nor the desire of reasoned men and women. I want to emphasize that Christ has set us free; we are indeed liberated by Christ. But not to do harm but good, not to indulge sin but to overcome it, not to satisfy my every whim, but to enhance the good of family, friends, the church and society at large.

Start With Where You Look and Where You Sit

Once again in Hebrews it states...

> "Therefore, since we have so great a cloud of witnesses surrounding us, let us also lay aside every encumbrance, and the sin which so easily entangles us, and let us run with endurance the race that is set before us, fixing our eyes on Jesus, the author and perfector of faith; who for the joy set before him endured the cross, despising the shame, and has set

Start With Where You Look and Where You Sit

down at the right hand of the throne of God. For consider him..." — Hebrews 12:1-3a

Further, we read in Ephesians...

"But God, being rich in mercy, because of his great love with which he loved us, even when we were dead in our transgressions, made us alive together with Christ (by grace you have been saved) and raised us up with him, and seated us with him in the heavenly places in Christ Jesus, in order that in the ages to come (where we now live) he might show the surpassing riches of his grace in kindness toward us in Christ Jesus."
—Ephesians 2:4-6

One key to freedom depends on our perception of reality rather than reality (from our world perspective) itself, and on our position rather than our possessions. For example, when a person has obtained great wealth or fame, we may see that the cares of the world are weighing them down so that they cannot enjoy their wealth, nor their fame. This is often seen in Hollywood, but also in the church.

How sad, since neither wealth nor fame is inherently evil, and in fact, more of it would probably be a blessing to many of us (especially wealth). However, if possessions possess us rather than the later, freedom eludes us. Thus, the scripture adjures us to make certain to look in the right direction and at the right person to avoid empty freedom (which, of course, is not freedom at all) that money and fame cannot provide to us. We must keep our eyes on Jesus. But why, and how difficult is this?

Well the why seems clear... he is our Savior, Lord, King, friend, should I go on? You get the picture, and the picture is exactly what the writer of Hebrews wants his or her audience to see. Look at Jesus...look at all that he said and all that he did and how he sacrificed for all of us so that he might bring many sons and daughters into his family. As we gaze at him, the one who died, and when looking on the risen and ascended Son of God, we realize that in time we will look much like him. We were created in his image and likeness, and thus we are destined to rule and reign with him. Yes, we are joint heirs of salvation. All that God has created including the earth and its fullness, given by the Holy Spirit, belongs to the heirs of salvation. We are the heirs of salvation.

Looking at Christ and focusing our mind and intentions on him is not difficult when we remember that we are sitting with him in the heavenlies...right here and right now. He is not far away from us, for we are in him and he in us. We are sitting together at the table of the Lord, feasting daily on the Father's presence, close enough to hear each other's heartbeats.

Let us not forget one of the most accurate but saddest indictments on the Pharisees (the very zealous but misguided spiritual leaders of the time of Christ). They did not know the scriptures (their true meaning) nor the Power of God (Matthew 22:29). They were looking in the wrong place. They were looking for a kingdom in this present world rather than one in the Spirit. Thus, as believers, we can now look intently into Christ without fear, but with anticipation and in faith. We know that we are being changed from glory to glory, for his glory, the glory that he shares with us as his sons and daughters. (John 17)

Fully Alive

Freedom, from a biblical (and common sense) view, recognizes that we can never be fully free independent of relationship. As newborns, we begin life with a primary narcissistic view; we are self-absorbed, naturally and necessarily by God's design. As every healthy parent will attest to, the goal is to see our children grow to maturity. Over time, they should go from being self-absorbed to having the ability to share, to give to others and to see value beyond eat, drink and be merry, for tomorrow we can do it again if we are fortunate.

In other words, we hope our children grow up to become sufficiently independent. We want them to enter into healthy and satisfying interdependent relationships. True independence, where we withdraw from or only use others for our own satisfaction is never healthy, nor will it lead to freedom.

This secondary narcissism is in fact pathological, although it is frequently seen in the world in which we live. We were created by family, in community, for the family to give back to the community. This important point is often missed, even in the church. We need each other, and true freedom is found in healthy interdependent relationships, as we learn to love each other by grace in truth.

Beth Moore, a prolific writer and teacher is quoted as saying:

> "When we see ourselves as the center of the universe, we live in constant frustration because the rest of the creation refuses to revolve around us.[1]"   —Beth Moore

---

[1] *Breaking Free: Discover the Victory of Total surrender*, B & H Publishers, 2007, Nashville, TN

11

"To be free is to put justice, truth and service to others over and above our personal gain or our need for recognition, power, honor and success.

When we cling to personal power and success, when we are afraid of losing social status, then we are in some way denying our humanity; we become slaves to our own needs, we are not free." —Jean Vanier

"If a thing is free to be good it is also free to be bad. And free will is what has made evil possible. Why, then, did God give them free will?

Because free will, though it makes evil possible, is also the only thing that makes possible any love or goodness or joy worth having." —C.S. Lewis

Chapter 2

Freedom is Being Who You Are

In Paul's teaching to the Ephesians, (more on that below with help from my dear friend and mentor Dr. Ken Chant) he urges the church in Ephesus to remember their status. Although they are stuck in difficult circumstances, they are to consider the reality that they are dead in Christ, buried in Christ, raised in Christ, ascended in Christ, and are presently seated with Christ. Since we are dead, we are free from sin and its consequences. This leads many to ask, "Can we sin?" The answer is of course, you can, but you do not have to, and why would you want to?

In Romans 6:7-15 Paul addresses this as well. The fact is we can choose to sin. If our goal is walking in true freedom as a believer, and it certainly should be, then for our benefit and to please our Father, choosing not to sin is within our power. That is, if we remain focused on where we actually live; in the heavenlies, above the fray of the world. Does this then mean we will never sin? Well, I wish it were true, but again John the apostle, closest to the Lord during his ministry, states unequivocally...

> "If we say that we have no sin, we are deceiving ourselves, and the truth is not in us, if we confess..."   —1 John 1:8-9

In fact, we will sin (miss the mark) even though we are in Christ. We have a new nature and we are a new creation (Second Corinthians 5:17), and in this new nature, given to us by Christ through Holy Spirit, we have no sin. The old nature is now gone in Christ. We can still choose to follow the impulses of our old nature and will be tempted to do so for the rest of our natural lives. However, when we look to Christ, we can fully enjoy the freedom from sin and its consequences, all by his grace and the power of God that works in us.

Thus, freedom comes as we ultimately embrace who we really are...worm, slave or royalty? Dr. Ken Chant, my dear friend, has just completed a new book on the book of Ephesians.[1] With permission, I have paraphrased portions of his book, as they speak to the issue of freedom in such a wonderful and dynamic way. He states:

> "To actually come into the fullness of our freedom in Christ, we need...
>
> ### TO ACCEPT THE DIVINE DEFINITION
>
> ...of who we are."   —Dr. Ken Chant

As Christian people, we should bravely affirm what scripture says about us, which states that we are divinely righteous in Christ. Not that we progressively become more righteous, through much self-effort and

---

[1] *TREASURES FROM PAUL, Volume One, Studies from Ephesians,* Copyright ©2012 by Ken Chant. All rights reserved worldwide. To order Dr. Chant's excellent work, see www.booksbyvision.com

painful strain, but we are, right now, the righteousness of Christ. What God says about us in Christ is even more true than our life experience, or what others might say about us, namely, that the righteousness of Christ is always greater than my sin (Romans 5:17). This is true because...

I AM DIVINELY IDENTIFIED IN CHRIST

This was also underlined by John (See John 10:34-35), in which the people of God are called "gods". How startling that sounds! How can it be proper to call you or me a god?

The ascription "gods" was given to the people of God because...

THE WORD CAME TO THEM

That is true of everyone who believes in Jesus, for how can we believe until we have heard, and how can we hear unless someone has preached the gospel to us? (Romans 10:13-15) Problems arise when people stop with that. To live in the authority of scripture, we must keep that good word coming to us by reading it and meditating in it continually (Psalms 1:1-3). In fact, much of the work of Dr. Chant, myself, and pastors everywhere is to see God's people become lovers and livers of the word of God, not because it is our thing, but it is their right and privilege to know and live in and through the word of God fully, and yes, freely.

Notice how full of the word of God Jesus was! He was surrounded (John 10:24-31) by angry, savage men who were eager to kill him; yet he remained calm and was able to give them an immediate answer from an obscure passage of scripture (Psalms 82:1-6). The serenity, the authority, the victory that Christ displayed did not happen by themselves. Rather those qualities arose out of his absorption of the promises of the Father. He was, above all other men who have ever lived, a man of the Word. Further, in his life and ministry, Jesus was the most self and other conscience; fully aware of his surroundings, the world in which he lived, with a full and complete awareness of the Father and his will for him. We too, as we study the word and live in the freedom of the Spirit can be as fully aware as Christ... living life to its fullest.

Jesus read the scriptures. He absorbed them, he meditated on them day and night (Psalms 1:1-3), he declaimed them, he trusted them, and he knew they were the word of God and that they would endure for eternity. In this, as in all things, he set an example. In many ways the people of God, but especially Jesus, stood in the place of God. The judges were God's agents on earth (see Exodus 7:1; 22:28), hence they were called gods. Likewise, when you and I act in Jesus' name (his authority as ambassadors for Christ) and in harmony with the word of God, then we speak with the authority of God. That authority is such that should it lie in the divine will, we can command mountains to move! (Mark 11:22-24)

So in Christ we gain a divine identity, which Paul insists gives us a place in the heavenlies, gives us authority over all the powers of darkness, and provides a right of access to the very throne of God and all heaven's abundance. Therefore, scripture calls us "gods", and bids us to conduct ourselves accordingly.

If you are "in Christ", then you are the very righteousness of God! Further, you are more than a conqueror! Moreover, you carry the true image of your God on earth, bearing his name, possessing his authority, reflecting his beauty, and destined for his everlasting glory!

There is an ineluctable spiritual law that faith must precede practice. Many Christians fail to live victoriously because they break that law. They try to reverse it into practice first, then by faith. Before you can truly behave like a saint, you must believe that you are a saint! So we are required to say, "Because I know that I am good in Christ, therefore I will do good!" Christ presented the same law in his saying, "You will know the truth and the truth will set you free" (John 8:32). Before freedom comes knowledge. Liberty arises from revelation. Power in action is a product of the promise believed. This is such a profound truth, one it would behoove the reader to meditate on, and this theme will be expanded on in the conclusion of this work.

So, here is something we all want: freedom! We desire freedom to serve God and to love him; freedom to rejoice in his goodness; freedom in worship and prayer; freedom to live righteously and to walk soberly and godly in this present world; freedom from sickness, and from every dark work; freedom to prosper every day in the favor of God! In addition, how can we obtain that freedom? Jesus said simply, "know the truth!"

Therefore, before you start praying for some need to be met, or for some freedom to be enjoyed, you should take these two steps:

- Find out what God says about his willingness and ability to meet your need (that is, discover the truth, find the right promise); and then...

- Believe God's promise with all your heart.

Your knowledge and faith in the word of God is the initial key to all his wonderful treasures. A true "believer" heartily accepts the witness that God has given of himself and of his will in the scriptures. In particular, real faith requires acceptance of two things:

1. You must believe what the Bible says about Christ; and...

2. You must believe what it says about yourself. In fact, nothing can happen effectively on earth until it has first happened in the heavenlies; thus:

    - You cannot gain victory over Satan on earth until you have first seized the victory that is yours in the heavenlies; you cannot live in the abundant blessing of God on earth until you have first seized the treasures that are yours in the heavenlies.

    - Indeed, once you have positioned yourself in the heavenlies in Christ, and there grasped the promises of God, those promises will soon begin to be fulfilled on earth. Paul says this great work has already been done. This is not a promise. It is a statement of fact — "God HAS (already) blessed us with every spiritual blessing in the heavenlies."

See it again: all spiritual blessings — all the good things you have ever longed for and prayed for; every blessing the human heart could desire, and every kindness divine hands can provide; all the riches of glory, and all the stores of earth, restricted only by the larger purpose that the Lord may have for your life. Paul says that this great work has already been done. This is not a promise. It is a statement of fact — "God HAS (already) blessed us with every spiritual blessing in the heavenlies."

Do you say you have need of blessing? God has already blessed you! What has he given you? It is nothing less than "every spiritual blessing"!

Can you even begin to measure the profusion revealed by that statement, or can you ever exhaust that limitless treasure?

Consider it

In many ways, it is all in the mind. Thus, we must first consider the implications of Paul's teaching. We are indeed free in Christ, but to walk in that freedom we must (Colossians 3)...

- Consider or think about it, and...

- Render it (determine in your heart and act on it) as already done in Christ

- Remember it then forget about it... for to be free is to walk naturally in your new nature, which we can do in the power of the Spirit.

Freedom comes by revelation of knowing who Christ is, and who we are now, in him. To walk in that revelation requires the releasing of the past and any resentment or unforgiveness that we may have. We must also release our hurts and resentments and even our triumphs and victories. Of course, this is often easier said than done, it is a process of transformation, of forgiving and walking in obedience. But God is patient with us. Thus, our transformation may well occur with the help of others, friends, family, pastors and even professional counselors in rare occasions, but remember, this is often done best as we commune with the Lord in worship and participate with the Eucharist and as we live in a loving community. Then we are free indeed, which leads us to...

Freedom is Being Who You Are

- Taking responsibility (First Peter 2:16)..."act as free men, and do not use your freedom as a covering for evil, but use it as bond slaves of God." For... we are truly free.

- Again, remember, "It was for freedom that Christ has set us free; therefore keep standing firm and do not be subject again to a yoke of slavery."

The yoke of slavery does not keep you from heaven, but it does keep you from fulfilling a purpose or destiny in God. Willful disobedience, apathy, ignorance and the bondage of rules and religion will definitely hinder your walk with God, and your ability to be all God intends for you to be.

I AM

In Exodus 3:13-15, God the Father reveals himself, in response to the question of Moses, who shall I say has sent me, I am Who I Am... in some translations of this, it could also mean I Will Be Who I Will Be. This revelation of God to Moses was essentially the same words Jesus used to describe himself to his disciples and the people at large. (see John 6:48; 8:12; 10:7,11; 11:25)

Jesus said I am...

- The Bread of Life... the living word of God that feeds and nourishes us, and the provider of the daily provision we need to sustain life, and even abundant life on the earth. Further, he declared he is...

- The door to the sheep fold of the Father, to life eternal, the one who introduces us to the Father, and in knowing the Father we know all we need to know regarding our life and identity; our purpose.

- He is the Good shepherd, who brings us safely into his kingdom of righteousness, peace and joy in the Holy Spirit (Romans 14:17). Further...

- He is the way, truth & life, the resurrection and the life, the creator and sustainer of all that is...this is who the I Am is, and He will be what he will be.

That is, Christ had to determine, in himself, that he would indeed be who the Father had begotten him to be...and in similar fashion we must choose to be who we will be, once we have embraced our full identity in Christ, empowered by his grace and truth, his word and the Spirit. We can become all God intended for us to be, but it begins by finding out who we really are, and really believing what the Word has said about us; then acting on it with all our hearts...which is what walking in wisdom is all about.

Paul's Echo

Paul the apostle experienced many trials in his life, many obstacles to his calling. Though certainly not a perfect man, he persevered, because he knew who he was, and who he was not. In First Corinthians Paul states...

> "But by the grace of God I am what I am, and his grace towards me did not prove vain; but I labored even more than all of them, yet not I, but the grace of God with me."
> —1 Corinthians 15:10

Please note that grace, and knowing the favor or grace of God preceded his work...that is, knowledge of his gifts, calling and anointing came first. Yet I am sure that the knowledge of the grace of God did not happen all at once, but also progressively, as Paul had to journey towards wholeness just as we do. Paul grew in the grace and knowledge of his Lord and Savior Jesus Christ (Second Peter 3:18) just as do we.

Later, John the apostle wrote in First John...

> "as he is, so are we in This World"
> — 1 John 4:17

What a profound statement, for this must mean...

- God is love, so we are love in this world

- God is grace and truth; so we are grace and truth in this world, in fact, the only true grace and truth the world will likely see.

- God is life, and we bring the message of life to the world, as we preach the good news of Jesus Christ, savior of the world.

- God is light, and we are the light of the world, not hidden, but shinning forth as a beacon of hope to the world

- And...we are the door to Jesus who is the door to the Father; we are also to be good shepherds, purveyors of eternal life, distributors of bread, both natural to the hungry body and spiritual to the hungry soul...and of course...

This too is freedom, the knowledge that as he is, so are we, that we are who we are, accepted by God, loved by him, eternally forgiven, and able to freely give what we have freely received.

"What are your choices? Whom are your choices for? Not just for yourself. Chose now whom you will serve, and that choice is going to affect the next generation, and the next generation, and the next. Choice never affects just one person alone. It goes on and on and the effect goes out into geography and history. You are part of history and your choices become part of history."   —Edith Schaeffer

"Free will is not the liberty to do whatever one likes, but the power of doing whatever one sees ought to be done, even in the very face of otherwise overwhelming impulse.
There lies freedom, indeed."
—George Macdonald

Chapter 3

Keep Looking Up!

In James it states...

> "One who looks at the perfect law, the law of liberty, and abides by it, not having become a forgetful hearer but an effective doer, this man will be blessed in what he does."
> — James 1:25

James statement almost seems contradictory... for how can liberty and law fit into the same sentence? An attempted explanation follows below. Further, in James 2:12 it says this, "So speak and so do as those who will be judged by the law of liberty."

James refers here to the "law of liberty". The natural question generated by his statement here is, "What exactly is the law of liberty"? Remember as stated above, liberty is defined as the quality or state of being free. In seeming conflict, a law is usually something that prevents us from doing something that we want, or believe that we should have the right to do. Why then is there not a contradiction in this statement of the "Law of Liberty". Essentially, the reader is being bound to freedom.

James does not attempt to define the meaning of his statement (a common problem with the study of scripture in general). In order to fully understand his meaning it requires that we look elsewhere within scripture, which we have already done in part. We started our study with the scripture from Second Corinthians...

> "Now the Lord is the Spirit, and where the Spirit of the Lord is there is liberty."
> — 2 Corinthians 3:17

Wherever Jesus is, there is total freedom. Thus, beginning from the moment we ask Christ to set up permanent residence by the Spirit in our hearts, we begin the walk of freedom from freedom. It is a walk of freedom for we have been, past tense, set free from the law of sin and death. We can only walk in the freedom that has been granted by acknowledging that we indeed are free and by becoming bonded to him in love. Jesus is fully free because he loves all of us with an eternal love. We walk in freedom as we allow the love of Christ to permeate our hearts and minds, and act on that love in our relationships. Love is the law of liberty that we are to live in.

Once again in Galatians it states...

> "Stand fast therefore in the liberty by which Christ has made us free, and do not be entangled again with a yoke of bondage."
> — Galatians 5:1

Christ has set us free from the works of darkness and the effect of sin in our lives. He has also set us free from the Law of Moses. The law has only revealed our sin, and although the law is good, righteous and holy, we could never in our own strength keep the law. This brought us into a form of bondage. Sin brings us into another form of bondage. Both of these types of bondage have been dealt the blow of death through the blood of Christ.

To walk in freedom, we must fully understand the freedom that we have attained through Christ. Then we must stand and remain in that freedom, resisting the temptation towards the sin of self-reliance (sin) and the external restraint (law).

So what then is the law of liberty? The law of liberty is freedom from sin and the works of darkness, which has been granted to us by grace through faith when we turn from the world and accept Jesus into our lives. The moment we accept Jesus as Savior and Lord, we are immediately set free from the law that held us captive. Then we are released from the bondage of sin and are granted the ability to walk in total freedom.

The fact remains however that although we are set free from the law of sin, we are thereby free to choose to cast aside the freedom we have received through the love of Jesus, and return to the captivity of the past. Once again, I ask, why would we ever want that? Accept the fact that we have been set totally free and that sin has no authority over us. The law that Christ has made is that we are to be free. That freedom is the ability, by the empowerment of the Spirit, to love God (because he first loved us) and our neighbor, as we love and respect ourselves.

So, as a believer it is essential to confess our freedom, walk in our freedom, and enjoy the freedom that Jesus has given. We do so as we continue to walk in the perfect love of Jesus.

Man in the Mirror

The King of Pop, Michael Jackson, sang a song a few years back titled *The Man in the Mirror*. It was a song about change, and essentially, his message was that if someone was going to change, they had to take a good look at themselves, and determine to make the change... and change. Well, most of us wish it was that easy, to include no doubt Mr. Jackson himself, who was ever changing but seemingly never truly happy with the change.

Again, let us look at Paul's powerful statement in Second Corinthians, where Paul reveals that the focus of change is indeed in looking at oneself, but more importantly, in looking in the truth of God's word, the source of change.

> "But we all with unveiled face beholding as in a mirror the glory of the Lord are being transformed into the same image from glory to glory just as from the Lord; the Spirit."
> — 2 Corinthians 3:18

Paul starts his statement with inclusiveness, not exclusiveness. It is not me but we that become transformed. When we look into the face of the Lord with unveiled face through the word and worship, we are transformed. As previously stated, context helps our understanding.

A Tough Place

James, as did Paul and Peter at times, was writing to a church under pressure. He begins his letter by urging the leaders and members in general to "count it all joy" when you come into troubles... easier said than done.

A Tough Place

Obviously, the church in Jerusalem and Judea were under severe persecution, and the faith of the faithful was being challenged. James urged them to stand firm in their faith, ask for wisdom to endure, and to avoid the usage of anger to try to overcome the pressure of persecution.

Taking of revenge may feel sweet, but is never a strategy given us from the Lord. Instead of seeking revenge, or trying to endure in self-effort, he gives them something to do with the difficulty of the day. Take a look inside, deal with your own and not another's issues. Put aside wickedness (the generational sin or consequences of sin from the past) and filthiness (things we choose to do that soils us), and choose the road of humility.

Freedom is very much a soul issue. The Lord wants us to fulfill our purpose, our destiny, to have all we need for our journey (having prosperity) and health, which only comes as our soul is aligned with the soul of the Lord, or having a renewed mind. So, James once again urges us to look in the mirror. Look together with our brothers and sisters in Christ, not to judge for the purpose of condemnation, for there is not condemnation for those in Christ (Romans 8:1) but judge ourselves in light of the love and light of God that we will see together, as we worship and study the word of God, and respond accordingly.

Once you look in the mirror, with an open heart, you will see God...he is love and light, then we must allow him to lead in the paths of righteousness...it is worth the journey, leading us to greater and greater freedom.

"To serve God, to love God, to enjoy God, is the sweetest freedom in the world."
—Thomas Watson

"It is a fact that the Lord Jesus has already died for you. It is also a fact that you have already died with the Lord Jesus.

If you do not believe in your death with Christ, you will not be able to receive the effectiveness of death with Him — freedom from sin." —Watchman Nee

Chapter 4

Freedom through the Anointing

When Jesus stood to read from the scrolls in his home town of Nazareth, he was not doing something unusual. However, it was the first time he had read the scrolls after rumor of his message and miraculous ministry had begun. The men in the Synagogue knew Jesus from the time he was a boy... but the rumors, could they be true? All eyes were on him, as he read from Isaiah 61 (as read in Luke 4), but with his own minor, but significant twists. Again, we read...

> "The Spirit of the Lord is upon me, because he anointed me to preach the gospel to the poor, He has sent me to proclaim release to the captives, and recovery of sight to the blind, to set free those who are downtrodden, to proclaim the favorable year of the Lord."
> —Luke 4:18-19

Jesus may have been simply paraphrasing the passage from Isaiah, and the sections he did not emphasize may have been incidental. But assuming (which I do), that Jesus did nothing but what he saw the Father do, and that he was most intentional in all that he did, I find it interesting that he emphasizes the poor, healing, release from bondage and God's favor rather than God's judgment...though judgment would indeed come. He presented to the people good news, the time had come when the promise of the kingdom would be fulfilled, and the response was anger and rejection, for what Jesus was offering was not appealing to the powers of the day. Jesus' message was the kingdom, and his method was the power of love. All of this would become a benefit to man because of the Anointed One, because of the one filled with the presence of God had come.

In the passage in Isaiah that Jesus quotes from, there are some distinct benefits to the anointing. Included are comfort for those who mourn due to losses of various kinds, a garland to announce the reality that we are members of the Kings household with all the rights and privileges (and responsibilities) of royalty. Also, it provides us with gladness, joy due to praise, a new stature (oaks of righteousness) that is imparted to us in Christ and a place of service in the newly established kingdom. These benefits and blessings are granted to all who believe in the anointing that we have received in Christ.

The anointing oil was used to signify something or someone that had been set aside for God and his service. A person thus consecrated would know that they had one and only one loyalty, to the purpose for which they were consecrated. The reason for the anointing was to serve the King and to serve those whom the King brings into our lives.

In his presence, we have the fullness of joy and true freedom, and it is in that presence that God goes about doing what is further discussed in Isaiah 61. He rebuilds the ruins of the past. God takes the burnt stones of our lives, as Nehemiah and his team did in rebuilding the walls of the city, and makes it all fit back together again. All the kings horses and all the kings men cannot put Humpty Dumpty together again, but God can take the broken pieces of our lives, and for the sake of freedom, put us together, piece by piece, bringing healing and wholeness to us by his grace and power.

Whatever God's original intention is for our lives, regardless of how desolate and desperate our situation might seem, he intends to fulfill his intention, and does so intentionally. Areas of brokenness will be repaired, even the foundation of our lives, our families, culture, will be redeemed and repaired so that out of our surplus, not our deficit, we live and move and have our very existence. (Acts 17:28)

We Got It

In First John it reads...

> "But you have an anointing from the Holy One, and you all know ... And as for you, the anointing which you received from Him abides in you, and you have no need for anyone to teach you about all things, and is true and is not a lie, and just as it has taught you, you abide in him." — 1 John 2:20,27

We have his presence, his power, his Spirit living in us; no one needs to teach us about this (though we definitely need teachers). His presence, the anointing abides in us, and thus we are "fat", anointed, set aside and empowered. A picture of this can be seen in Isaiah. This often quoted passage by Pentecostal preachers is used to justify altar calls filled with sensationalism. However, it is not about laying empty hands on empty heads, but about the importance of training or discipleship.

The passage reads...

> "The yoke[1] would be broken because of the anointing[2]" —Isaiah 10:27

Israel needed to overcome the bondage they were in due to their own sin. To do so, they needed to become yoked together with Christ (take my yoke upon you and learn of me, Matthew 11:29) to be trained by him. The choice was theirs, be yoked with the Lord, or remain under the bondage of Assyria.

Today, we have a choice to make, we can be yoked together (get trained), and come into healthy relationships in the body of Christ, or suffer bondage. Christ has called us to freedom, not bondage. Christ wants us free, and has declared us as such, but the path to freedom is a disciplined one, at times a difficult road, but one that the Lord has called us too. Each day we must choose to walk in what Christ has provided to us...freedom. Freedom to choose Christ, his word, his ways, and to remember to render the old life (old nature) dead, and to declare daily we are truly alive in Christ, enjoying the lofty position of being seated with him in the heavenlies, far above principalities and powers, and thus free to act out of our new nature, the very nature of Christ, with face always turned toward Jesus the Son.

---

[1] fatness
[2] The yoke of bondage, in context, put on Israel by the Assyrians.

Chapter 5

Conclusion

Freedom does not mean we will never have bumps in life, nor that the walk we are on will be filled with roses and Champagne. Freedom comes from our position, which is seated in the heavenlies in Christ; freedom comes as we walk out a life of love, for God and others. Freedom is choosing to obey the truth of God's word, knowing that the greater one lives in us... greater than the devil, than sin, than sickness and disease, greater than anything... it is for the very sake of freedom that Christ has set us free. Let us live as free men and women. Freedom comes by having an eternal focus.

That eternal focus includes a mind that has been renewed living in the Spirit and following the Spirit's Irrefutable Laws.

An eternal focus keeps looking to Jesus, the author and completer of faith... focusing on following the Lord's will and ways is key to walking in true freedom (see Hebrews 12).

Freedom is walking in faith over fear, for we have life eternal now, in Christ. Thus, fear of life or death has been swallowed up in the victory of Christ through the cross, a victory we share with him and all believers. Of course,

Conclusion

we must use our freedom freely (1 Peter 2:16), that is, not for ourselves alone, but for Christ and others.

Living out freedom comes through freely giving all that we are for the sake of the Kingdom of God. (Matthew 10:8; Romans 6:7,22)

A Final Thought for Leaders Present and Future

The more vision we have for the future, a future filled with the freedom for which Christ has set us free, the more power we have in the present. Hope and vision ignites us. It is for freedom's sake that Christ has set us free... but freedom was always for a purpose. If a leader chooses a life of abandonment of self to the Lord, a life of true freedom, the journey will not be easy, but no true victory comes without a fight... and we have been fit for the fight in Christ.

For example:

- Moses — a man raised with privilege, impulsively responds out of time to real injustice, was thus rejected. But he fell in love with Hebrews, was anointed by God, chosen from childhood, preached deliverance with power, leading the people to worship and prepared them to possess the land for God's people. Then consider...

- Joseph — a chosen child, favored (perhaps spoiled) by his father; rejected, imprisoned, called, exalted, delivered; and God used him to rescue his family, a nation and a people group. Then of course there is...

A Final Thought for Leaders Present and Future

- David — rejected (some believe an illegitimate child), a faithful son, called, anointed, challenged and chased; becoming a worshipper, conqueror and king. And who could forget...

- Daniel — a man in the wrong place at the right time, gifted, rejected, called, anointed, declaring, overcomer, etc., and God used him right where he was planted. He prospered in spite of circumstances, for the glory of God. And we could recount many more.

As leaders, we often carry a level of burden that the congregation rarely understands. God delivers, to bring freedom, to fulfill purpose. That requires government, which people resist. As leaders, mature believers, we are required, and it is expected, that we rise above the criticism, anger, vitriol and rebellion... which is not always easy. Like David, we often ask God (or at least think it) for our enemies to get back, pressed down and running over a measure of what has been dished out... but the calling, anointing and vision of God compels us to continue. Christ presented the same law in his saying,

> "You will know the truth and the truth will set you free" —John 8:32

Before freedom comes knowledge. But not just facts and figures, for how many of us look in the mirror and deceive ourselves that we really don't need to lose the pounds we know we need to lose. Knowledge needs to be understood in our hearts, and when understood, acted upon... which is wisdom... and really freedom is essentially walking in the wisdom of the Lord.

Further, liberty arises from revelation. More than mere knowledge, a revealed mystery, that we really are

Conclusion

who God says we are and thus can be all God says we can be and do all God says we can do. This reality must be embraced by us, as God makes us aware of it, conscious of all God has provided for us. Revelation, when received, takes the very doubt out of doubt and fear out of fear, for we know that we know that we know... and in that place is freedom.

Finally, there is power in action, which is a product of the promise believed. We are free, but just as it is with the pardoned prisoner who refuses to leave his cell, we can only experience the freedom Christ has for us as we believe in the promise provided. As leaders or followers, freedom has already been provided for, but as in all areas of our Christian life, it has to be walked out day by day, in faith. Remember...

"It is for freedom sake that Christ has set you free"... reject every restraint, reject every lie, fight every foe that would try to steal your freedom... for we really are free, as we know the truth and keep our eyes on Jesus.

About the Author

Dr. Stan DeKoven is the Founder and International President of the International Training and Education Network, which serves in over 150 nations, with its programs including:

- Vision International College: Church Based Education

- Vision Publishing

- Walk in Wisdom Seminars

- International Association of Christian Counseling Professionals

- The Family Care Network

And, Dr. DeKoven is the founder and President of Vision International University, a distance educational ministry, preparing students in various fields of Christian Leadership around the world.

Further, Dr. DeKoven is the author of over 35 books and study guides in practical Christian living, which are an outgrowth of his extensive teaching ministry both nationally and internationally.

Dr. DeKoven is a graduate of San Diego State University (B.A. Psychology), Webster University (M.A.

About the Author

Counseling), Professional School of Psychological Studies (Ph.D. Counseling Psychology), Evangelical Theological Seminary (D.Min.). He is a Ph.D. candidate in Practical Theology with the University of South Africa.

He is a licensed Marriage and Family Therapist in California, Clinical member of California and American Association of Marriage and Family Therapists, and the American Association of Christian Counselors, Co-founder and Doctoral Diplomat from the International Association of Christian Counseling Professionals, and is a Certified School Psychologist and Christian Life Coach.

As an Ordained minister, professional counselor and educator, he is actively establishing educational programs in practical theology around the world, via his personal teaching/preaching ministry.

For more teaching by Dr. Stan DeKoven, visit his website at www.drstandekoven.com. His blog is updated weekly with fresh insights from the word of God. Visit him there and leave your questions and comments.

Some Other Books by Dr. Stan DeKoven

- Grief Relief: A Biblical Prescription for Overcoming Any Loss
- Journey to Wholeness: Restoration of the Soul (the big picture of God's plan and purpose for every believer)
- New Beginnings: A Sure Foundation (for new believers and discipleship training)
- I Want to Be Like You, Dad: Breaking Free from Generational Patterns and Restoring the Image of the Father.
- On Belay: Introduction to Christian Counseling
- Supernatural Architecture: Preparing the Church of the 21st Century
- Grace and Truth: Twin Towers of the Father's Heart
- From Hurt to Healed: Effective Christian Caregiving
- Prelude to a Requiem: Principles of Leadership from the Upper Room

Some Other Books by Dr. Stan DeKoven

- What Does God Want: Getting Your Life Focused on What Really Matters

For a complete listing of books available and for purchase of these and other books go to ...

Vision Publishing
1672 Main Street, E109
Ramona, CA 92065

1 800-9-VISION

www.booksbyvision.com

www.ingramcontent.com/pod-product-compliance
Lightning Source LLC
Chambersburg PA
CBHW061515040426
42450CB00008B/1630